Tout Noir Press
Twenty-Four

Tina Abena Oforiwa is a Ghanaian born, London-based poet and author. Tina is an avid writer and reader inspired by the works of Ama Ata Aidoo, Chimamanda Ngozi Adichie and Haruki Murakami. This pamphlet is Tina's first published collection of poetry.

Twenty-Four

Tina Abena Oforiwa

Tout Noir Press

TOUT NOIR PRESS

Published by Tout Noir Press
www.toutnoirpress.co.uk
First Published in Great Britain by Tout Noir Press 2017
Copyright © 2017
Compilation copyright © 2017 by Tina Abena Oforiwa
All Rights Reserved.
No part of this publication may be reproduced, stored in a retrieval system, or transmitted, in any form or by any means, electronic, mechanical, photocopying, recording, or otherwise, without the prior written permission of Tout Noir Press.

The moral right of the author has been asserted.
First published in England by Tout Noir Press.

Oforiwa, Tina Abena
Twenty-Four
ISBN: 978-1-9998258-0-5

Visit Tina Abena Oforiwa at Tout Noir press
www.toutnoirpress.co.uk

For all the women in my life, every Ama, Afia, Abena and Yaa; this is for us, for the journeys travelled.

Twenty-Four

Leaving Home

By Your Side	2
Letter to Akosua	3
Anansi Becomes a Man	5
Making the Cut	6
Home	7
The Departure	8

Lost in Transit

Higher Learning	10
Sister	11
Where Your Children Are	12
When He Left	13
Adults	14
Child	15
Rug Burns	16
Nana Baa	17
Father	18

Love

How You Love Me	20
The Need	21
Stay	22
Mmere Dane	23
Power	24
Subtle Warning	25
When the Time Comes	26
i	27
ii	28
The Kiss	29

Betrayal

Rotten Fruit	34
A Sign	35
Necessary Villain	36
Lonely	37
Lust	38
Suicide	39
For Ilham	41
The end	43

Honour

Swim	46
Zion	47
Not All of Me Shall Die	48
The Gold of This Coast	50

Leaving Home

By Your Side

The cock crows at 5 a.m. You were up since 4 listening to the silence. You know soon this will be a thing of the past.
You're a pair of sardines in a tin; she taps your leg and whispers 'Maabena, are you awake?' You nod, staring up at the concrete ceiling. It rained last night. You fell asleep listening to the pitter patter of water falling on the iron sheet, and to her, snoring beside you.

Your aunt is up singing along with the cassette, the wondering love songs of Daddy Lumba going on about how dangerous women are; you hear your father grunt his approval. Afia is the first to hit the shower. Since she has grown breast the size of pebbles she now sings about love. As for you two, love is found in bowls of maize porridge and fried doughnuts, you don't speak of the impending departure.

Soon you are out on the veranda in the shade. The sun lapping up against the concrete. She jumps in and jumps out, thrusts her hands towards the sky, right then someone takes a picture. The picture you will later carry like a passport in your purse. She will always look free, and you, looking in at her freedom.

She will smile more, laugh harder and you will wonder, how. London couldn't teach you to reach for the sun, but all the while she had it buried within her skin, her dark hue testifies to this. Years later you will kiss her palms and pray into her hands and she will laugh. Never understanding that *akwaaba* was the scent of her fingers greeting your face, a gentle reminder that this, is home.

Letter to Akosua

They predicted I would forget. Supposed that, 'One day she will wake up at twenty-four and we will only be a daydream, fragments of a memory she picks up from the ashes of her night out in the Big City.' So now when I come home my cousin asks:

Do you still remember us?
'My name is Akoossuua Daarkuuaa', she said slowly. Stretching the syllables to source out if my English ear could hold the weight of my mother tongue.

Do you still remember us?
You are littered with the sounds of a million car horns, kayayo girls selling plantain chips and peanuts. The repetitious calls of ice water, the morning call for tea bread, you, are Alhaji K Frimpong and his Cuban Fiestas. Racing between cars as orange earth stains our church dresses, to nestle in wait of the sounds of Amakye Dede.

Do you still remember us?
You are the scent of heat rising from the ground after rain. The drum beats of the passing funeral procession as grandfather bows his head and children scurry indoors before the masquerade. The bitter sweetness of palm wine we steal away on Christmas morning. The bitter squint-eyed taste of Kola nut before the dawn. You are the last drop of gin giving ancestral offerings.

Do you still remember us?
Peeping through the slit of the door as grandfather loosened the wrapper around grandma's waist and she cooed, you giggled. She had never known another man, nothing like us.

Do you still remember us?
'My name is Maabena,' I quietly declare, with a voice that almost resembles yours, although we both know I am not half the person I used to be since I left. Still, I try. Holding your memory like clay formed beads around my waist, and when I expand out,

I find you nestled in the gap of my mother's teeth when she smiles.

Do I still remember?
   I open my arms and you enter its fold, our bellies touch and I whisper: 'Yes Akosua. Yes, I still remember.'

Anansi Becomes a Man

Over the phone you were giddy,
you said Kwame's voice broke like empty barrels of Calabash,
at last, he is now a man.

He holds his own in the midst of elders,
commands attention in the house
and expects extra meat in his soup.

At night, he peels off the bravado, cooing sweet nothings
into Linda's ear, forms circles around her navel.
He loves her, you're certain.
He said he wants to plant small colonies in her womb.
"Of what?" I asked.

"Of ant hills in the Savannah." We both laughed.

With all his manliness, he still washes grandma's feet.
Carries them in his hands like jewel-encrusted stones.
Prays into her cloth for good fortune and mercy.
In silence, over the static, we both agree.
Indeed, he is now a man.

Making the Cut
(There are things we fight to forget that will haunt us forever)

Between your legs was a burning highway
smouldering lava oozing down your thighs.
He will later try to hold you, caress the spot and you will hate
him.

Amina said it was worse than pulling teeth,
mouth gargling blood, eyes rolling back and finally
a blackout.

For days, your father's face will emanate a radiant awe.
The women of your house will congregate around your bed
and speak of your bravery.
Each face will look like a betrayal.

Your mother's eyes will avoid yours.
Your face will be an open terrain of vile discourse.
You will not hide your pain but wail till the ghost of her own
wound is reopened.

But they chant that you are pure.
That hollow well will never be a minefield to set men off,
it will be quiet.

Doused in the memory of this day it will hide.
Wait.
Close the door.
Light a match and if he dares, set him on fire.

Home

Home, is a quiet voice in a cupboard in the attic of the house you resided in at five, where the old rug still lies holding your scent in its fibres, waiting. It's the noises coming from the secluded room that housed the old man and his ramblings about a war.

Home, is the cracks you chipped away at on the wall, during your daydreams of a yellow bird carrying you across corn fields into cotton-stuffed clouds. The smell of damp from the curtains your mother made one random Sunday morning.

Home, still houses the ghost of your grandfather, sitting machete in hand on the veranda, waiting for boys who dared to tread past under the hut you had your first kiss

filled with blurred expectations, it rained, as if thunder clapped between your thighs so hard you were convinced you would die right there if this wasn't love.

Home, school days playing Ampe, Chaskele and Pombo, mouth dripping sugar cane and fan milk down your chin. It could never get better, never, ever, ever, until that day you met him, and that year he popped the question and you said

No. You were yearning for something larger and home was becoming a prison.

Home, in that room your sister's water broke.
In that room you spoke of the impending abortion.
The walls kept your secret but she couldn't, so you fled with everything except a suitcase and shoes, delicate feet splintered and bruised leaving home, a burning bush behind you.

The Departure

We leave, hands outstretched balancing expectations in our palms towards an iron bird.

Kissing old hands begging for blessings and favours from an earth which owes us nothing.

We leave, with our shoes on our head to feel the heat of the soil which regrets our departure.

Our wives weep, our husbands know we will never return whole we must give everything for a dollar, a pound, a little yen.

We leave, children in the care of uncles we can't trust and aunts who look the other way.

Our mothers we hear die crying our names but it's the sacrifice we make.

We leave, because to stay is not enough, this earth can't offer enough, this dirt is just dirt, dry land where nothing grows.

But even as we leave, we kiss the ground and carry the dirt in jars. We arrive, only to question why we left.

Lost in Transit

Higher Learning

I can't explain why our father left.
I remember the mug in the kitchen filled
with half a cup of coffee, an ashtray with
half a Marlboro stick, its fumes still lingering.

Weeks after he was gone his CK cologne
could be smelt everywhere on everything,
reeking of his absence.

Mum took to knitting on Mondays,
Bible study on Tuesdays and on all the
other days would sit in the darkness,
the light from the TV flickering,
reflecting her loneliness.

In this land, he could leave.
Her dark hue was no longer beautiful.
The weight of her love was breaking his back.
Oh, but what about Accra?
The nights in Kumasi making love to
Fela's blues?

Over the line, her sisters pray, curse,
dissect his reasoning, repeat in three different
languages that she wasn't to blame.
"He is a man and men leave," they say.
Our ears pressed behind the door
we ate those words, didn't we?

That Monday your teacher asked about our father,
apologised in a monotone way that these things
happen and you aren't to blame.
You shrugged, voice now soiled with new wisdom
"He is a man, and men leave."

Sister

That August on the journey from Tema to Takoradi,
our mother's left arm hanging leisurely out the window.
Her oversized sunglasses perched atop her head, bright
burgundy lipstick denoting some foreign opulence.

You parted supple lips, giving birth to a sound
you'd been bloated with for over a decade:
"ɛhenfa na yereko?"

Not so much question but the mere utterance.
The impromptu advance of language pushing against your
tongue, parting your lips like a lover, with sensual ease.

What was it, child?
In that second language had its fingers in your mouth,
feeding a new nuance, a new currency of exchange, a new way to
say: I have arrived.

Was it the trees?
Their effervescent green after years of concrete streets?
Perhaps the sweltering heat that lined your thighs,
sticky like Japanese rice on chopsticks.
What was it?

After fifteen years of void, darkness hovering over your insides,
curbing the tongue towards lighter more palatable sounds, then
suddenly, there was light. How did you feel in that moment?

Mother didn't flinch, she didn't notice the furrow of your brow,
the shift in your disposition as she replied, 'We are going to
Takoradi.'

You wanted to nestle back in the comfort of English, didn't you?
To swallow back your words, attach no meaning to, 'where are
we going?' But you couldn't. And by God I noticed.
Oh I did, I did, I did.

Where Your Children Are

We reek of foreign.
Of hotels with grand chandeliers in the lobby.
Of women who wear perfumes made in Paris,
shoes with Italian names and carry South Korea in their purse.

We reek of loss.
Shadows amid crowds searching for familiar faces like ours,
familiar faces of which there are none-
perhaps only in the night light when we walk swiftly with no
clue where we are really going.

We reek of belonging.
Tucked away in the crevice of Shinsaibashi, dancing
at 2 a.m. to the sounds of Fela Kuti and Prince Nico Mbarga
singing, Sweet Mother. Thoughts of whom we have not
forgotten only placed on pause for a little while longer.

We reek of desperate.
Cash beating between breasts, pulsating between thighs
to build mansions back home we can call paradise
through these hellish moments.

I bet your mother never knew that after bon voyage came
decrepit hotels and men who don't care that your last name
means warrior.

We reek of lonely.
Quiet days indoors, waiting for a phone call to speak to siblings
three of who are already married and the others who can't
understand why you haven't come home.
And what, do you tell them?

When He Left

For the first time in years
you allow your hands to search the inside of your thighs
and imagine how he was able to leave.
What made your softness different from the others-
bitter in his mouth?
How often were the nights you laid awake-
counting the many ways he said goodbye
while the baby screamed down the corridor?
Or knees bent, crouching on the bathroom floor
letters drenched, black ink running down pale skin.
And now the baby is the spitting image of him.
Such cruel beauty.

Adults

The adults in our family are still learning about love and marriage and what these two conditions entail.
I heard my mother whispering to my uncle to be more involved.

"Sit her down, talk to her sometimes," she said.
"About what?" he replied.
"About anything, about nothing."
It's been 15 years, but he still doesn't get it.

Last week, we heard he was having an affair with a German woman. His wife found an exchange of nude pictures in his wallet and his response? A cold silence which stretched further than the memories she has of the kind man she married.

Mother is convinced that it is something in our culture which causes this barricade of emotions. The furthest their parents had gone to talk about love, was that a woman is blessed to marry a man who holds her sincerely in his heart.

So, what about the others?

I fear to talk about us, the ones born out of this aloofness.
The ones for whom love is a myriad of emotions encouraged by Disney movies, fairy tales and Hollywood.

What do we do when we become, the others?
God knows I can't stand silence and the mere mention of a loveless hand against my skin boils my blood.

Somehow, mother is convinced that for us, it will be different.
We shall all marry white English men is her solution.
A remedy she slowly loses hope in whenever sirens draw closer and we know it's our English neighbours at it again.

So, I ask, what do we do when we become, the others?
And her silence tells me clearly, nothing.

Child

There are things that were screwed up before you were born.
Things that were orchestrated to bring you pain and uncertainty.
So now you fight.
Every day since you were a child you have been fighting to understand why things turned out as they did.
It's not your fault.
The grown-ups fucked it all up, only to later retreat and leave you to pick up shells, to piece together what they broke.
They screwed each other up right and proper.
But nobody takes responsibility now, nobody dares to understand how we arrived here.
They have played their parts in creating an uncertain future for you and now they retreat to God.
They wipe their hands clean and tell you to go pray.
But as your knees hit the ground and your voice trembles, pleading for understanding and clarity,
you're reminded of the beginning, when things were good.
When their pockets were filled fat.
When they would pay visits to your home and laugh with your mother.
Slap hands on thighs and promise the impossible.
They would reach in their back pockets and take a crisp red note saying, here child, something for tomorrow.
They had robbed you then.
Giving you what was already yours, what never belonged to them to give.
What did the grown-ups really teach us?
That the future is an uncertain place.
A trap set by their hands
A cage built by their lies and meddling deeds.
But you child, are a bright ray of sun.
A fire blazing in the forest.
A fierce sprinter.
You are strength they never foresaw.
And now you have arrived.
You are here.

Rug Burns

All conversations with our mother ended with a long sigh. I was certain it was because she was tired of cleaning offices, washing other people's mugs and cooking other people's lunch. She pulled me to the side one night, said all of that was easier than the memory she has of leaving Tema, arriving on the streets of London to be greeted with the news that her father had died two days after her departure, and the last thing he called out was her name.

It eats out her insides.

My father left her on a Thursday afternoon long before you were born. She crouched over, cried into the rug so long her face was someone else. Your father left her also, for not knowing how to let go and let him be a man. She was afraid of revisiting rug burns, and quietly, so was I. The only one for whom her knees would meet the rug with laughter, was her father. He was a kind and honest man, she said. Right then I erased the conversation I had with grandma earlier that summer, when she lifted her dress to show the scars of her rug burns.

Nana Baa

They laid your body out
a live carcass.
So, what happened next?
The vultures came to feed.
Your daughters protested, your sons held back tears.
Boys never cry, not on this land.
The inscriptions you painted on the ground
became a mantra.
What was it you said?
Love is open hands, closed eyes.
Love is open hands, closed eyes.
Now to that rhythm they bow down and kiss the orange earth.
The cracks and lines each a mark of some sacrifice,
some weighty promise you laid awake for,
some night you craved those dark hands giving and not getting
back love. How?
How did you carry the weight of a man like barrels of
water on your shoulders and expect nothing back in return you
soft
delicate
creature.

Father

At six, you were the figure of a toy soldier I kept under my bed. You would never grow larger than all my hopes bottled up, so why did you do it? Implant a dream you knew would never amount to much, and your excuse? You were young, but so was she.

At nine, you were a shadow dancing around a fire with ten sets of eyes bedazzled by your father as he told stories of your youth. A lifetime ago of innocence which no longer remembers you.
But I remember.

I have your eyes, is what your people say.
Your face is etched onto mine like engravings on a stone.
I stare at the reflection in the mirror asking, who am I?

I heard you eat sushi now where you are.
You dance to the beat of a foreign sound, make love to another in that same, soft, empty promising way.

Sometimes mother cries.
I hide my face.
Your features rest in my hands. I cradle you in myself.

You are a bright beam of light I will never grasp.
A lie of love I have told too many times.
Someone should have said sooner
you are never coming back, father.
You are never coming back.

Love

How You Love Me

There are a few things I know to be true.
I leave myself exposed easily enough to be effaced.
We are rivers running in opposite directions trying to
flow in sync.
You are strong, and I am not.
I wear culture on my sleeves, afraid that without its seams
I will unravel apart. You are free.
I've felt the dirt on my face, the earth in my mouth,
I know intimately what suffering tastes like.
You taste pain between my thighs and yet you swear it's sweet.
I am a shadow lurking in our home trying desperately not to crumble.
Our children bear your incandescent spirit.
My mother said I would frighten you away with my insufferable habits
yet even through the nightmares, you've stayed.
The rough of my hands is from grappling at things that begged to leave.
In bed, crossing streets, at my father's funeral;
your hand has never left mine since I met you.
I have travelled for months without speaking,
at times, my loneliness haunts me.
You occupy my thoughts with talks of love and possibilities
I fight to believe.
Your father loved your mother deeply, showed you how to
love a woman.
My father set himself on fire, my mother watched him burn.
Every time we make love, I cry.
You lift my skirt and lick the wounds of cigarette burns,
scars from my lonely days,
how do you do it, take all this pain and love it like art?

The Need

Our bodies

are

ageing

aching

longing

praying

pleading

to

touch.

Stay

I kept you somewhere deep inside me
an unspeakable joy.
Left you in the background of life just hovering,
a soundtrack slowly fading -
only to at once resurface on a rainy afternoon
a bright luminous light blooming in my living room
encasing my hallways with laughter and leaving stories untold
on my sheets.
I can't seem to spit you out or cut you off.
Your roots extend through everything.
The smile of my children.
The flat on Mill Hill with the frost stained glass.
The church off old Kent road sings your favourite hymns
every Sunday morning.
When I stand naked examining my flesh, I see your eyes.
I feel your hands, your lips whispering praise on my skin.
I hold myself, adoring me for you.
I know, it's those warm nights, those nostalgic days and
reminiscing afternoons that keep you here-
that makes it impossible for you to disappear,
fade, shimmer in the distant mirage like a vision.
But you don't want to leave darling, do you?
You don't really want to go.

Mmere Dane

Love has the amazing quality of making
you feel invincible.
Like you are the most important entity at
the very core of the universe
holding all matter together.
Like a waterfall at the edge of Everest.
Like a dandelion in the wind.
Love makes you warm.
But I am a difficult woman to love.
An impossible being to ground, so love,
what do you do with something as flighty as I?

Power

Girls like you carry whole histories on their lips.
Make it bitter to taste but hard to look away.
Your face is both strange and familiar.

You remind him of crossed borders,
succumbing to beating Djembes,
Talking drums, calls of the village crier
and this city.

You can never be soft
fragile
delicate
or forgotten.

Your face is a memory of a place he aches to find.
At night, he performs rituals to forget,
stretching his palms across thigh, belly and back.
Searching mouths which can't pronounce his name
without stutters, pauses – breaks
in intonation and nervous laughter.

So, he scrubs you off–
diluting your scent with Italian musk, French cologne
and an English Rose whose delicate features
he can't remember.

His attempts at playing blind weighs heavy,
digs fingers into his sides.
His lips turn to ash with attempts to forget,
but every whistle
every siren
every Pentecostal hallelujah
the market women's belly filled laughs
every echo of sound,
reminds him of you,
Nana Ama.

Subtle Warning

How do you deny a man who puts his knees to the ground and prays for your heart?
Do you cut him down like a tree in the evergreen and pretend that in the absence of others his pain makes no sound?
Do you create a tomb in your mind and deposit all talks of possibilities?
Or as flighty as your nature is, open yourself to others for whom love is not a requisite.
Darling, for how long will you leave yourself open?
A body with a cannon in your belly waiting to explode.
Do you know how much energy it takes for a man to love and what did you think- that others will love you with that same vigour?
Those hands stretching across your frame, a terrain of his possession.
What did you think?
That others would pray over your stomach and wish to make a woman of you?
What fool taught you that love resides everywhere with everything and why, did you believe them?
I guess all the while you were waiting for stars to align and trumpets to sound, but love is quiet
a flicker of light streaming through a lens to create magic.
Daughter, slow the voices in your head, not every man will love you, but there is still hope and a home to be made in the heart of a worthy other.

When the Time Comes
(For Kwame)

Guide her to the room where you learnt that a phone call to a friend was better than a bottle of gin or a pistol in your mouth.

Show her how the high windows exposed a light you were sure had been burnt out. Then teach her how to smile, the way you were taught by your father: from the inside.

When darkness seeps in, light a fire and sit beside her.
Hold her hand and remain there till sunrise. Don't utter a sound. Let your silence speak volumes till her sadness has no room to manoeuvre.

Allow the pictures on the wall to tell of how far she has come and praise, praise, praise be to God, she has many more sun rises to conquer.

Digest everything she says about boys, school, friends and things she's ashamed to even remember. Don't say it's a phase, don't tell her to pray, tell her instead how proud you are.

Let the baritone of your voice become a rescue siren.
Let the sounds of your footsteps announce that a friend is coming. Let her see you broken and human, something she finds herself in and teach her culture.

To understand why our people dance adowa and speak in proverbial tongues. Why our mothers sing while they sweep compounds and our fathers only cry when their mothers die and now look to her mother.

Kiss her feet and the inside of her thighs if you dare.
Spread your palms over her stomach and stand over her naked flesh but remember, don't touch her. Not until you are ready to be that man, when the time comes.

i

For the first time in years, I didn't want to write prose or poetry.
I didn't want to see life through the stream of a lens.
I didn't want to watch others re-enact their realities on a big stage somewhere.

God, I wanted to live.
To fold myself in your arms on those long bus journeys
trace my fingers across your lips and recite prayers into your palms.

My mother was right
I was in love.

ii

What did I love most about you?
It was the way you would say my name.
It felt safe in your mouth
grounded in your voice
eloquent and lovely
like it wasn't me at all you were calling.

The Kiss

Chubby cheeks soft like cotton balls
Lips taste like chalk
           takes
                   me
                         back
5yrs old picking clay from grandmas
Kitchen walls.

He reminds me of a time I had forgotten.
Tucked away in the corners of my mind
somewhere, in a room filled with
action figures, superheroes and
framed pictures of boy bands.
Mum's red lipstick, cap off, half dangling
off the dressing table.

In the background dad's old songs fill
the corridor rich and warm like the
groundnut soup mum prepares:
onions, pepper, garlic and parsley.
A fusion of spices enriches the air
soothing something deeper within.

I never thought a kiss could be like this.

Like, tiptoeing to reach the box of chocolates
at six which were completely off limits.
Like, tiptoeing to reach mother halfway
for a kiss filled with promise and regret.

Regret that this was all she could give,
not knowing this was all I required
and now you touch me like this.

Face pressed against your palm, soft
tender whisperings which send me back
to dad's hummings of Afrobeat sounds:

Fefe Naa Efe
What is more beautiful than this?

For a moment, I pause
lips slightly quivering, parting
to let your tongue which tugs at
my bottom lip, in, in

in that cupboard, playing hide and seek
knowing they would never find me, snuggled
in dad's oversized boots and coat, Old Spice
desperately clinging to me like to say,
remember the roads?

The village you descend?
The ones who never made it here?
Remember the song Grandma sang
the day you hurriedly left,
hurriedly left
hurriedly.

To rid yourself of the stench of gutters,
of uncontrollable laughter,
of the roar of motorcycles in blazing heat
shiny black bodies bathing under the blare
of an orange, God.
You edge my body closer, closing the light
between us.

The darkness from which I came
now screams behind me, in me
as our foreheads touch.
Your hand cups my cheek,
my eyelids drop.

But they have found me, sleeping in
the warmth of this memory adorned
with hangers, lips bright red tucked away
in the corner of this space
mum's laughter shattering the silence

as she scoops me into an embrace.

Into this embrace.
There is no greater memory than this,
then when you kiss me.

Betrayal

Rotten Fruit

I could feed you pomegranates and nectarines,
lace your lips with ripe mango and crushed berries
and you would still produce no sweetness for me.

A Sign

The day I can no longer love you, there will be
no more phone calls.
No more late-night conversations in the
blanket of darkness.
There will be no need for the TV at 2 a.m. with
thoughts of you in the background, or arguments
resonating a sadness too overwhelming to bear.
There will be no more, 'I miss you' notes on the fridge.
Love will not be made in the cracks of dawn
or at the setting of the noonday sun
there will be nothing.
But a long body of silence, lingering in the passage
making its way towards a room
where you will find me completely,
alone.

Necessary Villain
(Conversations with aunty Afia)

I could count how many times we made love with his mind in another room.
How many thoughts he had of leaving and the variation of ways it played out.
Each time I was crouched over, cradling his goodbye with his old T-shirt in my lap.
I smelled the stench of satisfaction as he uttered: "I tried but it could never work, you require too much and I gave as much as it's worth."
Each time I begged him to stay, grabbing the end of his shirt while he packed a suitcase.
In his version of our lives, I needed saving and he was the valiant knight giving love to something broken.
I guess that made him sleep easy.
What we would never talk about was the fact that his hurt began with his mother leaving.
How every woman's face bore the hallmark of her treachery.
That when he cradled me in the night I found the dampness of my hair from tears he shed whilst sleeping.
You see, I'd be weak if he needed me to be, play the villain if he required that of me.
I understood, sometimes my strength became too intimidating, a little like his mother.

Lonely

What are you so afraid of?
That you'll love the way your mother did?
Too eager,
too inviting.
A vase made to break.
A door left open down a vacant hallway.
A cracked window of an old house.
Nights alone in empty hotel rooms.
A siren in the distance.
A lone ranger.
An empty seat beside you.
Cold arms around you,
its Illicit promises over you,
its lies lucid, running riot in your mouth
and you,
so desperate,
so desperate
for love.

Lust

(A summer in Koforidua)

You are the last thing
I am supposed to think about.
The thing which makes mothers tell children
to wash their mouths out with soap about.
The thing which crawls under the skin,
sits dormant rotting away the insides.
My mother said you were worse than poison.
My name being dragged around the town
would have made old madams proud.
My father smelt you on my skin and set himself on fire
and even then, you fed me with dirty hands.
I fell asleep with your arms around me
woke up to the silence of an empty room
a slit in the curtain and sunlight dancing on my naked skin.
What I never said was how much I enjoyed it.
Everyone adores a sadist,
the hand around the throat,
the brute force,
your wife's call
and my quiet reply.

Suicide

Falling in love
  with a married man
is like falling off a cliff
  head first
hoping that beneath you
  is clear blue water
instead of the concrete surface.

It's bleeding
  from the inside
 by a knife you swallowed whole
   hoping to give birth
to something of substance
   something of worth
but always
   there's just blood.

It's accepting
  he will never be the one
Never hold you with both arms
  wrapped warmly around your waist
and breathe a sigh of relief
  into your bosom because you
are not his home.

When your tongue slips wet and
  wanting into his parted lips
you will search the roof of his mouth
  to find another's name
inscribed all over its surface.

You are not
   some star-crossed lovers
whose love was disrupted by the gods
   you are just, his mistress.

A body which is not a temple
   but a deposit
of the weight of lust he cannot bear
   the shoes of his father
he will never fit into
   and the face of his wife
soiled with years of memories.

Falling in love with a married man
   is like falling off a cliff
 head first
   and moments later,
colliding with the ground.

For Ilham
(حطام في لا, سلام في كن)

The conversation began with a stale silence.
Before you broke the cord and asked what made me
call in the middle of the night, and I still couldn't reply.

By the time I had gathered the courage to say thank you
you were saying, no, it was your duty.
But you don't understand, sometimes men can be cruel,
so good men like you deserve the thanks.

I began from the most appropriate time: the beginning.
When everything was dark and all I could feel was the pain
living under my skin. My brain all entangled like a telephone
cord twirled around a finger. I told you I was sick, inside.
You said it didn't matter.

Let's start from the beginning when I could hardly speak.
And you were trying to know my name, where I came from and
how I ended up here. When you would hold my face in your
palms and all I could do was cry.

The beginning.
My brain all entangled like a telephone cord twirled around a
finger and you began the arduous task of detangling.

You washed my hair, my hands.
Taught me that love could be made with eyes, fingers, lips that
trained me to smile and laugh.

Our past is for the past you said,
but somehow, in the midst of the washing of hair and hands, of
trained smile and laughter, my past gained ground.

It began, louder.
The snickers, the cruel laughter, the finger of blame shoved in
my face.

My children looking on with those solemn eyes.
My husband relishing the role of the victim,
and my mother, reminding me of what we were:
The Ghanaian girl, the German man.
This Muslim girl, the devil.

The end

An affair is like a party, eventually, the music stops and everyone goes home.

Honour

Swim

On the day you were born it rained.
Grandmother carried you in a cloth
over her chest to the river.
The child must learn to swim, she said.
Her limbs must flex against the tide
her lungs must create room for water
she must learn to drown.
She approached the bank and removed her cloth
bore her naked flesh to the river with the women
of our village behind her,
                      a dozen eyes towards God.
They called on Twieduampon Kwame,
the giver of life and destiny to bring you peace
from the tirade of tongues peppered with insults for
women like you.
She laid you flat in the arms of the river
beckoning the spirits of ancestors to follow you.
She knew, that your path was set for a land
destined to bring you more confusion than harmony.
The women drew towards the water and each
extended a hand towards you,
a ring of apology and promise.
From every home, every street corner, every hut
came whispered prayers.
They gave thanks for the voice you would have.
The freedom you would wear loosely.
The pride you would bring back and the stories of culture,
legacy, and courage you would take of the women
who extended a hand.
The women wearing your skin,
their reflection in your eyes,
their voice in your vernacular.
For them, you would become a living tribute,
a testament to how we live.

Zion

Born out of a promise you can no longer remember.
Only that your father bled into the sand when you were a boy
and his blood swore that you would become something far
greater. So, you hold on.

Years later, you are learning the twang of a new language
a new dialect distinctly strange, yet delicious.
Its shades colour your speech, causes your tongue to do
backstrokes as you attempt to say your new name, Zion.
But your mother still calls you, Junior

a reminder of a boy not yet a man, a soul in transition learning
to unlearn itself, wanting to rewrite its origins but quietly,
fear finds a home in your mind and you're yet
still anxious of never living up to the greatness of your father.

The haunting prophesies which preside after each family
gathering as the big men shake your hand, stare into your young
face and you feel the weight of what you must become.

"What does it feel like to be a man?" She asked in your arms.
"Uncertain" you replied.

You will never tell her that you are afraid of falling away
desiring to adopt norms for which your friends will tease you,
for which all will look and mutter of how sad it was that he
failed his father.

Zion is in a strange place.
Between remaining a shadow and becoming a man.
The weight of a nation in his name.
The legacy of his father on his mind.
The hope of his mother under his skin
and a sea of black before him.

Not All of Me Shall Die
(For England)

We are the things around your necks.
The beads you wear on your waist.
The chimes you carry like chains around your ankles.

Our names are smeared all over your history,
as yours is over ours, enmeshed
like a grand oil canvas of the great Vermeer.
We both belong to no man's land, side by side.

Boots trudging through earth which belongs to no one
for a cause, we have both lost all comprehension of
between hating the enemy and hating ourselves.
What glory is there in unity?

What possible joy could there be found in confessing
we got it all wrong?

It wasn't a communist or capitalist thing
It wasn't oil or gas, dare I say, 'save the world from mass
destruction.' It was a fear, of ourselves.
A worry about our neighbour whose face we could not see
behind veils. Whose skin waned into a frightening night with a
heart of darkness.

It was a fear too rooted to be discarded, too abysmal to be
ignored, but we try, like vultures, now clawing away the truth,
pissing on our feet to purify centuries of deeds we can no longer
justify and what is left behind?

Epistolary accounts we revere.
Warnings we look past though the blood of our history speaks,
screams, questions for what glory, honour or anthem is sung for
those who die as cattle?

Still, we are the things around your necks.
The beads you wear on your waist
The chimes you carry like chains around your ankles.
We are memories only glorified in letters to wives and lovers.
And we are still here.

The Gold of This Coast
(For Ghana)

My people are a beautiful story
A dying breed of warriors
A living script of survival songs.
We are what the sea spat out after the arks triumph.
After colonial powers and freedom fighters
we are the lasting legacy of kingdoms.
Of Men who walked the breadth of the earth.
Of women who took up arms to go forward
till the last of us fell in battlefields.
My people are a beautiful song.
A living legacy of Osei Tutu and mother Asantewaa.
From adowa to agbadza, our bodies tell tales of the moon
marrying the sun
giving birth to twilights.
We are gentlemen paying heavy prices for women who
understand
the way to a man's heart.
My people are a beautiful struggle.
I'm speaking of the orange earth which remains fertile after
bloodshed.
Forests that blush green after their invaded,
crops which continue to harvest, continue to harvest,
continue, in abundance.
My people understand the art of love and forgivingness.
Understand that in my grandmother's hands lay the foundation
of blessings
imparting the wisdom that men, are not to be trusted but still
treasured.
From highlife to hiplife our bloodline runs riot
with the sound of the slums of Accra to the gates of palaces.
We are a memory which outlasts the notes in your history books
and we are still
living
in vibrant colour.

Acknowledgments

My Mother
My Father
My Husband
My Sister
My Best Friend
Thank you.

Find Tina Abena Oforiwa on our website via:
www.toutnoirpress.co.uk
and her socials:
Instagram @tinaabenaoforiwa
Facebook @tinaabenaoforiwa

www.ingramcontent.com/pod-product-compliance
Lightning Source LLC
Chambersburg PA
CBHW031510040426
42444CB00024B/1188